Foreword

Where have I worked? The industries have ranged from ecommerce/internet, entertainment, law, marketing, sales, teaching, and travel/hospitality. Some might see this as a negative when trying to pursue a career. Some of your prospective companies don't like to see the candidate jumping from job to job. They want someone who will last and be a leader for their own company. However in this case, what I mastered from this experience was being able to learn the "ins and outs" of acquiring new jobs easily.

From this experience, I will share the process with all of you. Gaining a new job, although energy reducing, has never been a tough task for me for one main reason—sales training. Simply, what it boils down to is using sales skills with the Human Resource department and your desired industry's department of choice within the company. This is what "THEY" don't tell you.

Introduction

Why can't I get a job that I really want? Why can't I even get to the interview phase of a job I desire? Why does nothing I have done work? Are these questions some you have asked yourself, at least once in your lifetime? Well if you've felt this way, I am here to tell you that you are not alone. There is a huge problem facing America's working professionals today. Even though it seems that holding a job is the hardest task in these tumultuous times, it actually isn't. Finding a job is much harder.

The majority of the US population admits to not knowing where they went wrong when pursuing their desired/dream jobs and most say they don't even know how to really go about acquiring it. Everyone has had this problem sometime in their life, unless they have accomplished exactly what they've always dreamed of doing-which amounts to only approximately 5% of the US population. This short book will explain, in 4 simple steps, how to get to the interview (and hopefully hiring) phase of a job you've always dreamed of. This can all be done via the internet—the most powerful tool you have.

While many experience this problem day after day, I have found a way to beat the rest to get my foot into the boss' door. I have outlined 4 easy steps to use. If followed correctly, you will be able to access any company's resources to make gaining your next job "as easy as breathing." All this is made possible by the internet and a phone. They are the only tools you need in getting the desired interview.

Just a little history on how this short guide book came about. I wrote this book after continually being asked by friends and family to help them and others with one of the biggest problems people are facing professionally—getting to the interview phase of their dream job. My research shows that the great numbers of unsatisfied applicants believe that the companies they have applied to just "trash" their resumes after they've been submitted. Many applicants state that they don't even get the opportunity to show their enthusiasm and personality because most employers don't call the prospects back at all—much less for an interview. Many potential workers have given up hope on the procedure of submitting their resume to the companies of their choice because they have nothing to show for it but constant negative returns over the years. The vast majority of people who apply for a job and are not contacted after their resume is submitted, just give

up, and figure, "They probably tossed it out," or think, "I guess this job is not meant to be."

I'm here to tell you that <u>what you didn't know is hurting you</u>. I'm here to tell you that <u>what you didn't do is paralyzing you</u>. That is why I have now put together this quick and simple guide for your professional road ahead. You will find it very easy to read and use time and again.

Some of you might be hesitant to the effectiveness of this short book. I understand. I am hesitant anytime I read something from some random person telling me how to go about doing something. If you're not questioning that, that's a problem and you actually should. You don't need to believe me yet. I have no way of guaranteeing it to you except by telling you this- **<u>Just try it out once and see for yourself</u>**. I am confident that this process works because I have seen it work for myself, as well as others I have consulted. All I ask is that you read on; you will be glad you did.

Following is an adventure book and a guide book in one. First you will read about my many adventures of attaining and trying different professions/jobs and the roller coaster ride I was on. Then, at the end, you will see a quick and practical guide book to help YOU get the job you want, much more quickly, based on my experiences. Enjoy!

Table of Contents

1. Where does the Greener Grass Grow?
2. Paper or Plastic?
3. Would you like me to check your oil and other fluids and tire pressure too?
4. Hi, you are one of the limited contacts that has qualified for our low price offer…
5. Scrambled or Sunny side up?
6. Kevin…go sit in the corner! You're on time out…
7. The Army and the Dallas Cowboys
8. Cart Boy
9. Plaid or Solid color V neck sweater or iced tea?
10. Cell Phones, what a concept!
11. Hablas Ingles? Europe here I come!
12. Clerking around
13. Wickenburg, Arizona
14. Howdy Pardners!
15. San Diego, California
16. Aloha, can I take your picture please? They're only $12.50 each…
17. The Gong
18. Want a SoBe?
19. Surf Break!
20. More stops along the way…
21. ***I want that job now! step by step guide***

1

Where does the Greener Grass Grow?

Hello

Where does the greener grass grow? I have to tell you Joe, I surely don't know…

Okay…instead of making this into a great big song and dance, I will tell it straight to you. The biggest problem I have ever had in my life is that I always thought there was greener grass everywhere else - other than the grass I was standing on (figuratively speaking of course). Sounds familiar? It wasn't much of a problem all these years as it was an irritation.

There was always this little spider biting at my heels at every turn in my life. I couldn't imagine not knowing what lied around the corner. Every chance I had, I tried to shake the little critter nipping at my heels. The faster I ran, the more I went tumbling down the wrong alley, out of balance and wobbly. Lost and having forgotten how I got down this far. I couldn't wait to be free of this wise guy of an insect trying to keep me from my happiness.

Later, I came to realize that this "critter" was actually all in my head. I had nothing on my heel except my shoe. I was always wondering…what unforeseen object awaited me around the corner? What opportunity am I missing out on that I haven't experienced yet? What person will I meet in the future on one of my adventures that will change my life forever? Needless to say, the critter in my head led me down a road less traveled. My road less traveled was called, "What's this over here?"

Sounds familiar? I am here to tell you that that road can be beautiful in the beginning. It's lined with great wondrous trees on a path of soft green grass leading you on your way with great plush areas to rest in as you take a break from following your dreams. Nice animals line the sides of the road squinting at you and making you feel like the king of the road while you wonder how lucky you are that you are finally free and off to the land that will lead you right to Heaven's gate on earth. "No more putting up with the things I don't want to anymore," you think to yourself as you smile and skip down the road, confident you made the right choice. You think of the letters you will write back to your loved ones, describing the beautiful scenarios that fill each and every day of your life while your friends and family are living in the "real" world. Won't they be excited to come and see you now? Won't they be jealous? Oh how life is beautiful…

Then one day you hit the, what I call, the Three Ups in life. First, you wake up. Then you throw up and finally, simultaneously and coincidentally, you grow up!

Most people stay in one place their entire lives. They get a job, buy a house, become friends with their neighbors, have families, consistently look forward to the weekends and dream of a distant far off place that will ease their misery and contempt for this God forsaken world we live in, virtually pleading for one day to meet up with the pleasures they are missing out on.

Sounds about right? Have you ever felt stuck with no choice but to do what you need to do, to make the money you need, to create the life that you want to live, to retire at a decent age, to die at middle class income level or higher? The only problem with that scenario is that somewhere around the middle of the road, many people stop and freak out and regret most of their decisions they made. It's called the Mid-Life crisis.

As for me, instead of planting my roots in a long-term "professional" (and personal) commitment, I hopped around the pond looking for something else. Little did I know that the vantage point, at which I saw my new perspective every time, was actually the same scene I would see over and over again but from a different angle (wink).

Have you ever thought to yourself, "Well, I've been here before…"? Imagine that feeling with everything in your life. Would you feel fulfilled? Would you feel that there's something else you need to keep you going?

I did and still do for that matter…

2

Paper or Plastic?

It all started in high school. I was having fun as most kids tend to do during that crazy, confusing time period, getting in trouble while ignoring the people that love me the most and finding friends that will accept me for who I was so we can carelessly and frivolously travel through life together happily, succeeding with each other as others fail, and looking to tighten the bond through challenging and un-escapable adventures. What?? Yeah I know…

While having fun with my best friends was a great time at the age of 16, it seemed we never had enough money for anything. Little did I realize that that was a long term feeling I should have learned to get used to since it was something that most people have to live with their whole lives until they somehow win the lottery later on, or find a way to acquire assets at some point. At this particular time, I really needed money (what's changed?), so I went out and got my first job. My family knew the General Manager of our local grocery store and he was kind enough to give me a shot to earn some real cash early on. I wasn't ready for the big time of course, so he started me with bagging groceries at the checkout lanes. I was ecstatic to say the least.

Note: That is how I've always been my whole entire life, thus far. I get excited at the beginning only to find out the reality in about 4 months time at which point I find a way to figure out an escape passage to a new land that will fulfill my destiny and allow me to find my happiness on the outside. More of that will come, so for now, back to the story…

I was making minimum wage plus tips. Tips, I say…usually it was when a kind older lady in retirement would be so nice to give me a buck or two after helping her to her car. Many customers would take me along with them just to make their lives easier, even when they could have easily carried the groceries out themselves. The physical work wasn't the problem. The problem was the hot Texas sun and humidity that went along with going outside and doing work in dark black pants, a long sleeve white shirt, and a tie. If you're not familiar with a tie yet, I will tell you that it's an evil apparatus created some time ago by some person that was intent on making men uncomfortable. I really wonder if the inventor of the tie actually wore the thing. Anyway, a tie is not a man's best friend and the last thing a 16-year-old kid wants to attach to his body is something that makes him look like his dad or uncle in the morning after breakfast. Not to mention in the heat while doing physical work, is not the place to be, while wearing a tie that constricts your ability to freely allow air into your body and to express yourself physically.

My thought was: I can't wait until the day that I can get my college degree so I don't have to put up with this mess any more. Funny huh?

Here we go…

3

Would you like me to check your oil and other fluids and tire pressure too?

When I turned 17, I needed a new job because I couldn't stand bagging groceries anymore. I don't know why I needed a job at all to tell you the truth, but I am sure it had to do a little with boredom and a little with never having enough money to hang out with my friends on the weekends. I guess I figured that if I needed to have a job, I would get one that would entail my looking cool and being able to work with a variety of people.

So I went to the country - don't ask me what my logic was at the time as I am sure I wouldn't have any idea. On my drive out, I spotted a popular spot called Rudy's Bar BQ. Everyone loved this place. It was always crawling (and still does) with customers, especially on the evenings and weekends. It was made up of a great Bar BQ restaurant and seating area and adjacent to it was a fully stocked convenience store and gas station.

I went in to see if they were hiring. Something kept me away from the Bar BQ side of the business and directed me straight to the counter where the cashier was inside the convenience store. I asked them if they were hiring. The cashier said, "Yes, actually we do need a 'Gas Station Attendant'". I said perfect. I pictured myself with a red shirt on, tucked in to a great pair of jeans with my towel in my back pocket as beautiful women pulled up to the gas pumps and needed my expertise in the skill of pumping unleaded gas without spilling a drop on our shoes.

I showed up for my first day on the job and fell in love with it. I was meeting people left and right. Part of my job, as I learned early on, was to restock the ice cold coolers with beverages only when there were no Full Service customers at the gas pumps. Little did I realize at the time that

that sentence would come back and haunt my existence. So, when there wasn't anyone at the gas tanks, I was supposed to make sure the ice cold coolers were always restocked, the floors were swept and clean, and the bathrooms were spotless for the Bar BQ customers. So as you can imagine, what do you think I did for most of the time as a Full Service Gas Attendant? That's right. I cleaned the bathroom and hung out in the cooler. When I was lucky enough that a full service customer would actually come in, I was overjoyed with excitement and could hardly contain myself. A customer would pull up and the bell would ring...ding ding, and I would bolt from inside the bone chilling cooler and defrost for a minute before putting the towel in my back pocket, and speed walk to the front door and out to the car port where the gas pumps sat to ask the nice lady what she would like done this afternoon to her car. The answers would generally be the same. "Could you fill it up please?" So I would try to act as professional as possible while pumping gas. The beautiful thing about this job was that our station was one of the handful of stations, left in town, that offered the full service option. So I felt special. I would spend my time there talking to the customers. That's where I first realized that I had a knack for understanding people on their own levels and creating an enjoyable experience through conversation for them. I never knew that was my gift at the time. I mean...who is actually conscious of higher callings at the age of 17 besides Tiger Woods and Martina Navratilova? So I continued living paycheck to glorious paycheck at my great job, never really knowing it wasn't all that great and never really dreaming of another career opportunity.

After pumping the gas, I would continue to wipe their windshields and check their oil to create a great customer service feel for the customers so that they would return. I wanted them to return. Because when they would return each time, not only did it mean a tip for me, but also more importantly it meant I could leave my ice cold jail cell in the cooler to interact with civilization again. With the continuous restocking and bathroom cleaning I was doing, anytime I was NOT pumping gas, the experience was starting to get to me seriously. My full year as a Full Service Gas Attendant ended quickly. I needed a change. I joined a telemarketing firm. To keep from mentally experiencing this new God forsaken job again, I will summarize it for you quickly.

4

Hi, you are one of the limited contacts that has qualified for our low price offer...

This was the most disgusting job I had ever had. The office was a total of two rooms. One was the smoking room. And the other was the smoking room, too. You would have thought they would have made one non smoking. But it was the early 1990's, still too early for Human Rights Violations, I guess...

In the two rooms there were two rows of yellow pages and phones that we would have to use to make calls to prospective buyers of our special introductory gift baskets. The telemarketing rep with the most sold per day would get an extra $5 on their paychecks for that day. I thought great...if I can sell the most for a whole year, I can pay for the hospitalization bills dealing from the continuous second hand smoke I encounter in the phone rooms. No kidding...you would walk into any one of the two rooms and you would be engulfed in a white recycled nicotine cloud that would suspend itself over your head the whole day and night. If you were lucky enough to get a 15 minute break to get some fresh air, you would experience what it would be like to get saved from the clutches of death's arms. I started full heartedly believing in God right about that time. Of course, this job was part time. Because thinking about it, if I would have had to work that job full time, I think I would have lived a short and fruitless life...because I would have definitely taken myself out of this world. I quickly realized that this was just another job just not cutting it for me. So I left...

5

Scrambled or Sunny side up?

Looking for a new opportunity to make smart long-term decisions to create a future filled with great earnings and long-term education, I joined the Army Reserve (with the co-signature of my parents of course, since I was only 17) ironically. Thanks Mom and Dad for making sure I knew what I was doing at the time.

Have you ever been scared beyond belief that you couldn't think, act, or make your own decisions? Imagine feeling like that every day for a week. Now how do you feel? Hold on, we're not finished… Multiply that feeling by 9 (which is the number of weeks you spend in boot camp for our beloved US Army) and you have the scariest lab controlled experiment imaginable. Why did I join the Army again, you might wonder? That's exactly what I said the first day of boot camp when I got off the "welcome" bus and stepped into Hell. That's short for Hot as Hell Fort Jackson, South Carolina. The worst time to be in this region is in the middle of the summer. As you can guess, I was chosen to attend one of our country's highly regarded penguin producing institutions at this exact time. Penguins?

To give you an idea of what boot camp looks like from a bird's eye view, imagine Human Individuals going into the entrance of a building with a sign that says "US Army" on it. Everyone (the soon to be soldiers) is dressed differently expressing their own unique and different personalities and mannerisms (which by the way is the greatest gift given to us by God and/or the Powers that be in my opinion) entering the building at different paces. On the other side exiting the building, you have the same colored marching line of humans or "penguins" marching in step behind each other with the same uniforms and showing no individuality or personality with which they entered the building with. You can't tell the difference between one penguin - I mean soldier - and another. That's the goal of the Army. March step-by-step under one order to conquer evil overseas. Unfortunately, the whole process does more harm than good in my opinion.

I have to say, though, that the greatest gift I received from the Army was the knowledge of the fact that we as humans are all in the same boat. No matter what you think you can offer in the boat, we're still all floating on top of an unpredictable sea together. What I learned most was that we had better work together to get safely back to land, even if it's for a temporary break, than trying to pursue our own egocentric goals on our own. You can apply this same lesson on small projects or national diplomacy and world affairs. The first person to stand up and show off, to rock the boat, will be thrown overboard. If we can only do this with world leaders, our life on this earth would be much easier. But that's a different story. A much longer and more complex one, at that, and something we perhaps should work towards collectively.

After my 9 weeks of hell in boot camp (which seemed to be like 9 years of being under communist control), I went back home to San Antonio. To the surprise of my friends and family, I looked like Arnold Schwarzenegger from the constant workout during that summer. Returning back for my senior year of high school was fun, after going through one of the toughest programs in the world. Graduating from high school seemed really simple at that point in my life, so my senior year was going to be really fun and filled with confidence. That is a great thing at 18, when everyone else is unsure of themselves. Sustaining that confidence with life's real trials and tribulations during adulthood is the real challenge. High school was nothing as I came to realize years later.

My senior year in high school was fun. I was dating one of the best girls I had ever dreamed of dating in my entire life. She was my best friend. We had real intimacy and trust and we took care of each other all the time. Little did I know at the time that I would not find that again for a long time. I was so happy, I felt like I was on top of the world. I never took anything else for granted and really felt like myself. I treated people like I had wanted to be treated all the while learning more about others and myself. By the end of the year, I was on top of the high school mountain. I had a great girlfriend, a handful of best friends I could trust, and I was popular with every group. In fact, by the time graduation came around and prom popped up, our year was over. For being myself the entire year, I was awarded the prize of "friendliest guy" of our high school. It was great. I felt I had finally arrived. Little did I know…I hadn't even left the gate yet. Nor had anyone else my age, but we were on our way into the great unknown that we all thought we had figured out already.

6

Kevin...go sit in the corner! You're on time out...

During my last year of high school I was looking to make extra money, thus I was looking for an ideal job that wouldn't take up my time on weekends so I could have that special time for the important events that would take place with my friends on Friday and Saturday nights (smile). My mother had always been my life coach and she always seemed to know what type of advice to give my brother and I at the perfect time. While looking in the weekend paper one Sunday, my mother asked if I would be interested in taking a job for the YMCA. It was after school on weekdays and I would work with the students across the street from my high school. She had heard that they were hiring from her friend. So, just as with everything in my life, I got excited in literally 30 seconds and started to imagine myself teaching kids the right from wrongs, keeping them busy until their mothers and fathers picked them up from school, and feeling intrinsically fulfilled from doing something great in society. So, as with other things that catch my fancy, I pursued this job wholeheartedly and passionately. I wouldn't let anything stop me in my path. The next day, I drove to the YMCA after school and filled out the application for the open job. I made sure to sell myself to the front desk person, even though they weren't even remotely interested in why I was really there, or in the fact that they had nothing to do with my being hired for this job 10 miles away; they were there to mark time until Friday so they could get their next paycheck. After filling out the application, I didn't receive a call back. My mother suggested I call them to see if they would interview me for the job. I persisted proactively and kept calling all week. Incidentally, this is where I first learned that you can have what you want if you get off your butt and go after it. After about a week of calls, I finally got a call back. It was from the Director of the After School program and she invited me in for an interview. I was ecstatic to say the least. I was told to come in the following Wednesday after school and meet with her. For an entire week, I read about the program and learned as much as possible on the YMCA so I could "wow" the director with my preparation and desire to be part of the team. I practiced interviewing for the position and communicating the unique contributions I could offer the program, the school and the kids. Of course this was all due to my mother's coaching, for I would have never thought to do any of that at the age of 17. Little did I know at the time that I would continue this same practice and process for the rest of my life, with other jobs. It was a good starting place for me, but I had no idea at the time.

Wednesday came around and I was ready. I had everything prepared and I couldn't wait to "wow" the director with my personality and charm. When I arrived I was ushered to the Director's office to be interviewed for the position. As I entered, there were already two other candidates seated. I was added to the prospects and sat down and wondered why there were two other people there already. I pushed that aside as the interview process started. I made sure the entire time, that I was the most passionate with my answers and most knowledgeable about the program. I don't think the other two candidates knew this was coming, but I blew them out of contention. I walked out proud with my head held high, knowing I was the next gift for the YMCA. Little did I know at the time, that all three of us got hired for three schools. And I'm glad I didn't know that, at the time, since that would have jaded my perspective on company goals at an early age and I was too young to be able to handle that sort of reality at 17. Eventually I got hired at my dream school working my dream schedule with elementary school kids in the After School program. I cannot say that there was anything I disliked about that job at the time. Besides the normal emotional behavioral problems of the children, it was smooth sailing. It was rewarding on so many levels that I felt I could do it forever. Well, until college of course. Because in college I could find more rewarding experiences and be set on my way to finding my dream career with a proper education and this one would only be a small step to get there instead of a larger perspective on my life calling, or so I thought at the time. Hence at the end of the year, I gave my two weeks notice and worked my last after school day…When it was over I walked out with my head held high and ready to take on the next level. But first, I had to go back to Army Cook School training so I could complete my training and be ready to be a combat cook for our great country.

7

The Army and the Dallas Cowboys

Cook school was interesting. That's all I will say. I learned how to run 5 miles a day, do pushups until I almost threw up, and how to cook chili mac and bake a pie from scratch. By the time I finished that 10-week training, I was ready again for something else. I came back to find my friends and the best time of my entire life. We had jobs, no school and were having fun just being ourselves and trying to find girls while out.

I started working at the Dallas Cowboys store in the mall since I couldn't go to school yet as I had come back too late from Army training after the school semester already started. I saw the ad in the paper. It was my favorite team and I thought, what could be better than this? I called and went in for an interview. Little did I know that my friend Heather's boyfriend, Joey, would interview me. He was just as shocked as me to see the opportunity we had right then and there. It was a no brainer. He liked me, I liked him, and we were friends. What could be a better professional work environment? After bullshitting for about 30 minutes he asked me to fill out the application and I was on my way. The next day he called me and said I was hired, that I could start the following day. I came in and started the adventure I will call the mall in SA days. We had fun every day. Across from us luckily, Heather worked with a handful of beautiful other girls at a lady's boutique store which sold dresses, jewelry, etc. They would eventually come to be our best mall friends. We would hang out all the time together from morning till night. We would share stories, help one other, buy each other food from the food court and live in harmony for about 5 months. I was the Assistant Manager there. When I think back on it now, I don't remember working a day during my tenure there. It was the perfect job. After the fun filled 5 months, it was time for me to go…

By the way, during those 5 months my closest friends James and Mark and I would hang out every night, no matter what our schedules looked like. One night turned into 2. Two nights turned into 4. Four nights turned into 7. Seven nights turned into 5 months. At the end those five months, we decided to leave home together and move to one of the greatest cities on earth - Austin, Texas. Our parents weren't too happy about that, but we did it after convincing them that we were going up there to pursue an education and a better life. Yeah right. We found a better life, in terms of fun, but education ended up being the last thing on our minds…who knew?

Somehow, I found myself able to get into school from the get go, so I feel I was lucky at the time. During that first year of school, I got a job in the mall. It was at a cart.

8

Cart Boy

You know those carts in the middle of the mall that insure their owners pay exuberant amounts in rent to sell diddle daddle items from specialty shoes, to sunglasses, to leather items, to the all popular Middle Eastern sea salt skin cleansers and creams? I wanted to do that job more than anything in the world. Why you ask? I have no idea, but I think it had something to do with my desire to be in the middle of the action where all the hot girls walk day after day in search of their new look as well as emotional cravings and justifications to feel better about themselves. I was there. No one would take me away from my post. I started the "career" at a great concept cart. It was called Gobi Wear, Gobi for the cold, rocky desert in Mongolia and China. Why the name? I am not sure, for it had nothing to do with the concept of the products we sold. But it was catchy nonetheless. The owner, which little did I know at the time, was an older version of me. He was entrepreneurial, bored, energetic, idea-oriented and a change agent (for himself). Earlier, he had gone to law school and by the time I met him, he was already in a pre mid-life crisis at age 30. He quit his high paying lawyer job, and along with his wife, started buying solid white t shirts and coloring them different colors at home to create an inventory plethora of solid colored t-shirts. It was genius. I couldn't think of one place I could go back then to get a good quality solid colored t shirt, much less in different color options. I was on board. They hired me instantly and my first day of work was the following Saturday morning. They were expecting me and I told them not to worry, I would be there on time.

The Friday before that Saturday, my friends Mark and James decided to go out for a night in town (which would make 5 nights in a row that week…hey we were 19, give us a break). With a little arm-twisting, and no persuasion by them, I was in. It was a special night, that one night. We had met up with James' beautiful girlfriend and her friends, and it couldn't have been better. We were in the company of each other and with beautiful women by our sides. We drank, danced, drank some more, danced after that, and then shimmied together into the night. It was a late night, really late. To keep you from the boring details of the latter part of the night, I will zoom to the next morning. Somehow, with God's graces, we made it back to the apartment in one piece around 5am, yes…in the morning. I was supposed to get up for my new job at the cart by 7am, only two hours after. You can probably guess what happened. There weren't cell phones back then to get a wake up call from anyone, and I didn't remember to set the alarm either. I don't even remember if our phone in our apartment worked because for some reason, I didn't wake up on time. Instead, I woke up accidently to go to the bathroom around 10am. There were no messages, no calls that I heard and no persons that looked alive in the apartment except for me, and I wasn't fully up yet if you can imagine. After visiting the restroom, I stumbled back to bed. About 10 minutes later, as I was nodding back off to sleep, I remembered that I had a new job I was supposed to be at. So I lay there thinking, "Oh screw it", I don't need to go. I'll get another job. How hard is it to get a job at the mall anyway at my age? As I was trying to get back to sleep something inside me started eating at me and I thought I would throw up. I am not sure, to this day if it was my conscience or the 151 and vodka I had the night before which might have started mixing together to make an exit. Whatever the reason, I told myself that I should get up, take a shower and head up to the mall and take my chances. After about another hour of slow motion movement, I found myself able to get out the door and into my car. The drive was horrible, to say the least. All I could imagine was the owner's eyes and the trust he put in me, and the disappointment he would feel in the person he thought would help him in his new venture. I felt awful to say the least. It didn't help that the ounces of liquor and beer were still in my belly from the night before and weren't helping how I felt about myself. When I got to the mall, I made my way down the long escalator ride, which seemed forever at the time, and down to the cart I would start my short career at. As I turned the corner I spotted my boss and his wife, of course they both had to be there right? They were folding shirts, talking to fill up the time between the arrivals of customers. I managed to create a smile of some sort and said "hey guys, how are y'all doin?". They just stared back and looked at each other, and the wife put her head down and started folding shirts while the boss went to the register, ignoring me. I felt the pain and disappointment, and I was really sorry in my heart. I told them how I got caught up with friends the night before and how I made a mistake and if I could have one more chance if they would please help me out this once. I continued to plead with them, trying to convince them that they wouldn't be sorry. Eventually through the power of my persuasion, or their desire to have me there since no one else was hired yet, I got to stay for one more chance. They told me that I had to come in the next day to open so that I could learn the procedures and get the keys, etc. I said great, I will be back. They said, AND you can stay today and we'll teach you the other parts of the job so you'll be ready to go after the weekend. I smiled and said, "of course, whatever you need me to do, I'll do it". So I asked for a favor if I could get something to eat and drink before I started my shift. They said yes. I made my way up the escalator to the food court. As I turned to see what was there, I saw the restroom sign first. I made my way there. The closer I got the faster I started walking. Eventually, I made it and turned the corner and entered the second stall (the first one had someone in it). As I was ready to do my business, I felt a ball of acid and whatever else roll up from my stomach and into my mouth, as I unleashed fury from the night before on the poor toilet below me. It was the best thing that could have happened. After about 10 minutes of losing my fun from the night before, I cleaned up and made my way back to the food court. I got myself water and an orange juice, and decided to just get back to work. I wasn't in the mood to put anything solid in my stomach. That was the start of a great adventure at the cart. I learned a lot about sales, courting customers trying to avoid you in the mall, and how hot the girls were that worked at the other carts. That's where I fell in love for the first time in my life. Her cart was next to mine. Her name was Jackie. My life would never be the same again…well until she dumped me…and my cart closed down since it wasn't making much money and the owners decided to go back to living the high comfortable life. I found myself alone…without a girlfriend…without a job…in the middle of the mall after 10 months of absolute fun. I had nowhere to go. As I was leaving, I saw the Eddie Bauer store across from me. It was teaming with life and energy…and I said to myself…let's give that one a try…I know I can fold shirts at the least…what else will happen in this unconquered casual wear world up ahead? I was giddy with excitement as this new opportunity was rolling through my unsettled mind…

9

Plaid or Solid color V neck sweater or iced tea?

Have you ever been to Eddie Bauer? I think it has changed a lot now but back in 1994, the store was all about the casual look and the outdoors. Every time I went in there I felt that I should pick up some stuff to go fishing or camping in. It was an interesting concept and one that I would never forget. Wait…no…I would forget it, I would forget it quickly, because it wasn't as exciting as it looked. Hmmm…had I felt this feeling before? I'm sure I have and I am sure I will again.

The only memory I have of that store is folding shirts and jeans constantly. I am a people person. I like to talk to as many people as possible (well it used to be more of a desire when I was younger and working at that store) and folding clothes all day doesn't leave much time for the socialization part of the job which was evidently my favorite part. Every time I would try to leave my post, the manager would bring me back. I think she had a GPS location finder on me. No matter where I was, she found someway to find me and get me back in the proper role for the company since they were paying me a whole $7 an hour, which was a little over minimum wage and one that I was reminded I should be very grateful for since I am an average citizen with no real potential to make more money (being sarcastic).

At the time, all my best friends were working at Chili's Grill and Bar as waiters, making a lot of money ($40 a shift in tips) and they had a new opening. So I made my move. It was time to play Server…

Would you like to start off with an iced tea or a margarita on the rocks (with a smile)?

I first approached Chili's in Austin, Texas about a month before the biggest week of our lives at that time…Spring Break. That was the biggest week of our lives, by the way, from ages 16 to 23. Nothing would beat that week during that time. Nothing was greater. No situation could ever beat that transcendental party atmosphere. Even if aliens came down to earth and landed on our front porch and had a beer with us as we picked at the guitar and had friends over while we exchanged views on the universe and secrets, it still wouldn't match that great feeling the week of Spring Break would give us for those 7 years or so. Anyone that has ever been on Spring Break knows what I mean. It's a week of total debauchery and fun where anything goes. No rules (well not a lot anyway), and all fun. No way were we missing it…

Anyway, I walked in to the interview having prepared and studied up on the menu (since my buddies coached and tested me the night before). I met with the GM there and I blew him out of his seat with my knowledge, passion and desire to be the best dang waiter Chili's had ever heard of. I had the job in my hands. It was like taking money from a 5 year old. I was thinking of what I was going to do the rest of the day to celebrate and was getting ready to get up and leave when the GM said, "I just have one more question for you"…and I said, "sure", he went on to say, "Can you work the week of Spring Break?". I said, "Yeah…ok…but I would love to, you know…since this is the position I want and I want to show you how much of a great job I will do, I don't want to miss an opportunity to show you that in the beginning of course…and I think I can do that…but well, I am not sure if the guys (my friends already at Chili's) told you, but we're off for the week from school and we are planning to go to Cancun… our flights and reservations have already been made, but I can see what I can do to get out of it…but what do you think? Is there anyway we can make that up somehow? I will be ready to go right after Spring Break… I know I can train as quickly as possible beforehand and then be ready to pick up all the shifts when I return. I can be the guy that helps all the other waiters with the shifts they want to give up and then transition into my own schedule to help out the team…what do you think? I know it will be worth it, I guarantee it…"

Chuck (the GM) looked at me and smiled, and now I realize why…he saw that I was still young and didn't want to hurt my feelings I guess or maybe he thought I was a con artist, whatever the reason, he stared at me as I waited for the final sentence before I got my job and he said, "Call me when you get back from Spring Break and we'll talk about this opportunity again…then…ok?" All the energy left my body and I was down to a normal human being once again. I was down and upset but I collected myself and said, "Ok, thanks a lot for your time, I really appreciate that, and I will definitely call you when I get back". So I had to endure the painful, abusive, mentally tiring job of folding shirts and jeans for the next month or so while I waited for Spring Break. It was the longest month in recorded history I recall. After folding approximately

1002 shirts and 921 pairs of pants, I quit two weeks later. To make ends meet, I got a job at a Pizza place making pizzas. It was definitely one of the worst places I had ever been hired. I hated it. I was stuck behind the oven all day and I couldn't leave and talk to anyone. I lasted one week and then quit that job and then worked odd jobs for another couple of weeks.

Somehow, I finally made it to Spring Break. My friends and I packed our things with our big ol smiles and headed for the airport. The next week would be paradise on earth…and we didn't want to come back. I won't bore you with the unbelievable details of fun we had since that's for another story. Unfortunately, that week went by really quickly and we were back in our living room staring at each other as we dreaded going back to work the next day in our depressive states. As we thought about the next week or so exhausted from our fun, my friend turns to me and says, "Well, 51 weeks till spring break". We all started laughing and I said, "I can't wait…"

After a few days of getting my body and mind back to normal working order, and feeling the pain folding my last shirts, I called Chuck the GM again. Luckily, he still had an opening for me and I went back in. That was the start of a fun and chaotic (at the same time) job experience. My life would never be the same again…

Have you ever had a server job? If you haven't, I will tell you that it will change your whole perspective on work, what it takes to make money, will increase your patience and agility, and will make you very appreciative of every waiter you meet in your life thereafter. The training at Chili's was so intense that I almost quit. It was physically tiring and mentally degrading. You had to remember a lot of different things at once and be able to keep track of 4-5 tables and customers at once. I eventually made it through with a little encouragement from my friends who had already gone through the same torture about a year before. Once I got my own shifts and tables, everything started to get greener. I started to see every table and order as an opportunity to make money. I had the power (or at least I thought so at the time) to increase the amount of money I made by making sure I was on time, and as quick and responsive as possible to each and every customer that came my way. Generally, things went well. To be honest, I wasn't a good waiter. I was really friendly and I made up for my bad timing and inconsistent deliveries of food with my personality and love of people.

Chili's was really more of a social setting where I made a plethora of friends instantaneously, which I thought at the time, would be great. Little did I know it would create an exponential amount of drama that I would have to deal with for the next three years. I think everyone should wait tables once in their life. But not too long…honestly…you will never learn to take as much shit, as when you are a waiter at a restaurant. I say don't stay too long for this reason…the problem is that your customers are there to eat. So you can pretty much assume that they're hungry. People differ when they're dealing with hunger, but most commonly, your customers are irritated and not in the best mood until they load up on fat, starches and protein to settle their stomachs (and issues). So to add to the fact that your job is already hard since you have to literally "wait" on people hand and foot, you get more irritable people in your area every 10 to 15 minutes or so since the idea is to get as many customers in and out of the restaurant between the normal operating hours of 11am to 10pm.

Unfortunately, your shift doesn't end until they stop seating your section with the hundreds of crazy hungry lunatics. When the sky opens up and your section finally closes and you can breathe again, you end each shift with the arduous task of having to clean your section and the tables spotlessly. Following the normal 4-5 hour shift, you're in a unique state of being mentally and physically drained - you're absolutely exhausted and wound up at the same time. So you have two choices… One, you can go home, take a shower and relax on the couch while watching TV or reading a good book to keep you mentally stimulated and in the learning process. Two, you can wind down at a local bar where you grab a drink with your fellow coworkers and other local waiters in town who can share your pain and their stories as you all drown your sorrows and try to elicit a smile.

Looking back, I would advise most of the people to go with option One, 75% of the time if they can. The reason for that is due to what I learned and got to see first hand. Option Two unfortunately creates a situation where you get in the habit of drinking after EVERY shift, after about a month of working at an establishment. One drink becomes two, two becomes four, and four becomes nine and so on, as one shift becomes two, two become two a day, those become every other day, and you're working way too much at this kind of position. To finish the story, you go drink at the end of every shift now, and once you're done and ready to go home sloppily, you go pass out at home (or the other waiter's couch) after somehow making it there and of course you sleep late into the next day. When you check your wallet the next morning and realize that you spent half the money you made the day before on that same night at the bar, you get depressed and call your job to unfortunately pick up more shifts. The process becomes a never-ending cycle and you end up hanging out with social alcoholics for the entire time that you wait tables at that restaurant. Once you realize that you have to get out of there because your new family of alcoholics are crazy, you make your break for another restaurant since you have the skills and experience now.

Once you are lucky to transfer out of that first restaurant, you find that there are a few jobs out there you can get quickly. So you move on to the next place and you think I am going to do it differently this time. Naively, you find that the new restaurant is organized and operates the same way if not almost exactly. The same types of people come in hungry and the same stress is created for the different variety of waiters there. So one shift becomes two, two becomes five, one drink after work becomes two, two becomes eight, one night becomes two, two becomes five nights, and so on and so on. You get the picture. That's why I say now if you try being a server to make some money that I still think is a good experience, try to do it through option number One.

Quick note: I made a lot of great friends there and wouldn't trade the experience and fun for anything. I went on to work at two different restaurants. The first one was on the lake in Austin, Texas and I thought it would be much different and more intrinsically rewarding. Of course I was wrong even though the sunsets on the lake were unbelievable and unbeatable. The last place was called the Hula Hut. Idealistically thinking, I thought…well I would be on another lake and in a Hawaiian atmosphere, what could be better? Same thing, different location…but the money was better there. Advice: If you're going to wait tables, pick more expensive restaurants.

10

Cell Phones, what a concept!

One thing I didn't mention before, while waiting tables, was that I became irate after a while, just like the customers I was waiting on generally because I was getting so sick of the job. The enthusiasm I once had was finally gone after about 3 ½ years. Therefore, I decided I wanted to use my new found upselling skills I learned from being a server, and put them to use in this new world of cell phones I was seeing slowly explode around me in 1997 to 1998. Luckily, just as I was about to get fired because of my attitude, I landed a job with a cell phone company. It was called AT&T. This of course, was before the company was called Cingular and then changed back to AT&T, by the way. The phones have changed dramatically since then as well. They are much easier to sell nowadays.

I went to an open interview with AT&T at the time and somehow landed the job. It wasn't until later that I realized my skills in persuasion and sales are what were landing me the different jobs in the different industries, but that's to be discussed at a later time. It was a great experience because I had to stand in the middle of the mall, at a cart again coincidentally, as you know how much I loved that experience. It was awesome…I talked to everyone that passed by about these new cell phones that weren't as big as a brick from your house and were fun to use and to carry around while enjoying the freedom to communicate to whomever you wanted to at anytime from anywhere. It was awesome! The phones back then were bigger than they are now of course without any great extras to get. The phones were just able to call someone else for a limited time before you had to charge them again quickly while games, applications, media, other options in general, and text messaging were unheard of. It was hell to say the least. But customers bought them left and right, and an industry started to grow. Little did I know at the time that I was seeing history in real time and an industry was starting to develop literally, into a monster. Who would have thought people needed to communicate that much to each other at random times during the day for no apparent reason other than to keep in touch with each other? Interesting...

I can't complain about my experience there. Little did I know that I would return to this industry later in my professional life. I spent about a year there before finally and barely graduating from college with a degree in Psychology from the University of Texas. Hook em horns! Europe here I come...what? Oh yeah... I decided to go to Europe for 2 months. Why not? I still had financial aid money and a desperate need to see other things. Off I went...

11

Hablas Ingles? Europe here I come!

After graduation, I had another kind of itch. NO, not the kind that entails a visit to the doctor's office, but one of pure adventure… I decided to use all my remaining money and a credit card to go to Europe for two months before I started "working in my professional career" whatever and wherever that might have been for me. But it wasn't time, so I didn't think about it. It was time to get back home, do research for a week, and then fly off across the water to find myself or someone else for a bit, whatever would keep me occupied the longest. Luckily, my cousin was an ex adventurer who happened to now live in Paris, France. He told me he had some standby passes I could use and he would let me stay with him before I got going. It was perfect. Right in the middle of the action is where I would end up and who better to get me going on my crazy adventure than my own blood relative cousin who was much crazier than me and had the experience to share? I headed down the road with my oversized backpack, confidence, undersized wallet and a sense of logic.

I hit seven countries in 2 months. I never really stayed longer than 4 days in one place for it was impossible to do and I had nothing to stay for in any of the cities (except in Greece, I would come to find out too late, after I left like an idiot). The first was of course Paris. It was so beautiful but the people were really rude. I never saw so many nationalists look down upon Americans for God knows what reason. I thought we were friends? Aren't we? Weren't we? Anyway, I started to see the charm of France from Paris to the French Riviera. It was beautiful. It was time to move on though after about a week there. I had a plan, but I wasn't sure where that plan would take, except that I was as giddy as a teenage girl going to prom for the first time.

My next stop was Italy. I decided to go first to every country I always wanted to see and leave time at the end, if there was some, for the other countries that were on page 2 of my mental 'places I gotta see sometime in my life' list. I took an all night train from Nice, France to Rome, Italy. It took forever. I decided that I should go in style, so I booked a sleeping room in one of the cars of the train. At first it sounded like a great way to travel, sleeping my way through the night, dreaming of the all the Italian girls I would meet, as I felt the cool breeze from the Italian night seep into the car as it played like a lullaby keeping me sound asleep. Ummm, it wasn't like that at all. At first it was fine, as I entered the car and there were four bunks with fresh pillows and blankets. No one was there, yet it seemed maybe I was early. I waited until five minutes before departure time and still no one had entered. So naturally, I thought, "Great, the car is all mine, what's better than that?" I picked the lower bunk on the left side of the car as you enter. As I lay down and started thinking of the taste of Italy, the door to the car opens up and a gargantuan man of I'd say 350 plus pounds enters the car and looks at his ticket, makes sure he's in the right place, smiles at me and says something in French. I nod my head politely, as I put my head back down on the pillow. Through my peripheral view, I see him contemplate if he should take the upper bunk or the lower bunk and I close my eyes and think, "please make the right decision" I don't want the drama of a larger man falling through the top bunk and landing on the bottom while I am on this stress free trip". As if he senses my feelings on the matter, he makes the decision to take the lower bunk and lays down on the lower bed. I take a look at my watch and there is two minutes left until departure. As I ease back into my relaxed mode, the car doors open again and two gentlemen enter the car about 30 something years old, and split the remaining bunks in the car as they say hello in English, but with an accent. I said to myself ok, it was too good to be true. The train eventually starts to roll on the track and I somehow nod off to sleep. About an hour later I wake up suddenly as I can hear the train squeak its breaks and speeds through the night. I thought we must be in southern France by now. I couldn't wait. What a trip. As I was trying to get back to sleep I could hear the large man beside me start to snore. It was so annoying. I couldn't get the sound out of my mind. He wouldn't stop. As I am trying to get that experience out of my mind somehow, a sickening smell wafts through the air and down to me. It smelled to be a mixture of bad body order and unchanged socks (and anything else) from above me. I took a look up there and I noticed his blackened white socks still on his feet, thank God, hanging over the top bunk above me, and I could just imagine where this guy had been before our cozy random trip together. Anyway, I thought positive and put it out my mind and decided it was time to get back to sleep so I would have the energy to see Rome. As I tried to go to sleep, I kept rocking back and forth from the train slowing and speeding while feeling the cool breeze, which was a welcome addition to the trip, until that same cool breeze would bring more of that horrible smell from above down to me in an unsolicited fashion. As the awful smell would disappear and I would close my eyes again, I would start to hear the unpleasant snoring rhythm of the fellow beside me. I started to unconsciously count how many separations in sounds he had between each snore and outlet of breath, I guess kind of like counting sheep, but it felt different. After about two hours of this constant back and forth feeling of being shuffled between hell and hellfire on earth, I decided to go outside and watch the country fly by while I had a cigarette in the middle of the night. It was more peaceful on the edge of the train and outside the cab. I felt at peace and started thinking of great things to come. I look to my right and about two cars down is a lady on the deck like me. She sees me and I look at her and then back out at the land. It seemed like two seconds literally, when I turned back to see her on my right about ten feet from me. I couldn't believe it as I jumped a little, startled about what just took place. I figured I was just really tired and I might have changed the time-lapse mechanism in my brain in the last day or so. As I looked at her approaching, she asked me for a cigarette. I gave it to her and she said thank you. I asked her where she was from and she said "Roma" as she walked away just as fast as she had arrived back towards the direction she came. I am sure I had a perplexed look on my face as I shook my head in confusion and finished off my cigarette. I went back in and managed to sleep, not soundly of course, but enough to get me through the next day. As I was floating into dreamland, I thought to myself, I am never taking a sleeping car train ride again.

The next day, we wake up as we pull into Rome. I got out, went to the nearest cheap hostel, put my things on the floor and passed out. I didn't wake up until the next morning about 6am. I stayed awake and read until it was light outside. Rome was great. I saw many great things, met many people and saw all the things you should see there, including the Vatican. Everything was greater than it was on TV, especially the coliseum. After spending two days there, I decided I would go to Venice, the city of romance, by myself. I arrived there and had some ice cream…the best ice cream on earth by the way. If you're ever there, make sure you do that… I can't explain it, but you'll understand once you try it. Venice was beautiful. On my second day there, I was lucky enough to meet a girl there on a trip with her parents. They were from America too and we hung out all night there. It was like God sent down someone for me to experience the romance of Venice with the boats, the food, the wine, the feeling of being in love (even though neither one of us was really in love), and being far away from home. We were in an eight-hour paradise, both idealists I am sure, thinking back to it now. Eventually we said our goodbyes and never saw each other or talked again. I got up the next morning and got back on the train and headed to Greece.

On the way down the right side of the boot of Italy I met a young girl, a little younger than me at the time, who lived in a small city towards the bottom heel of the country. She told me to get off with her since I was on vacation and she would show me around her city, and then take me back to the train station after we were done. I decided that was the greatest idea I had heard the last few days and took her up on it. I ended up staying all day and we had a blast. She showed me where she grew up, where she went to church, where she went to school, the beach she hung out at and where she liked to eat. It was innocent and unique. We said our goodbyes and I got back on the train at night and headed down south some more. I couldn't get all the way to the city to catch the ferry so I had to stay the night in another city…a city of high criminality, I heard as I got off. I found the nearest hostel, locked the door and went to sleep. All through the night I could hear locals yelling, screaming, partying, God knows what else. I woke up the next day and headed right back to the train station. After two hours, I ended up in the city with the ferry to take me across the first island I would encounter in the country of Greece, Corfu.

Corfu was heaven on earth. Really…it was beautiful, remote and off the left coast of Greece. I spent three nights there at a place they call the Pink Palace. It's a hostel with all kinds of activities and various types of travelers from all over the world. It was the best time I had on the whole trip, I have to say. It was the first time I would take part in an international toga party all night, the first time I would hang out with Australians, South Africans, Canadians, Spanish, other Europeans and Asians all in one place. It was unbelievable. When you show up, they give you an introductory shot of Uzo, the national drink (basically an alcoholic black licorice taste). From that point the travelers would take those shots every 30 minutes or so for the rest of the trip. Between shots, we (my new friends and I) managed to get in a few games of volleyball, tour the island on scooters, and go cliff diving in the middle of the Mediterranean, where they would literally take you out on a boat about 30 miles out to a free standing rock cliff rising out of the water randomly out in the sea. The cliff was 50 feet high. You could go to a higher point if you wanted, but I decided 50 feet would be enough to feed my ego. After praying and feeling the pressure from my "new friends", I finally held my breath and jumped as I started to think about my funeral. Somehow, I hit the water and floated back up to the surface to hear the screams of my newfound family. Feeling good about myself, I decided that was enough for one day and spent the rest of the time resting on another rock watching others feed their desires for unadulterated adventure. Once we got back to the hostel/resort, I crashed and crashed hard. I woke up the next day, after spending a total of three days there, and got on a ferry to get to the mainland of Greece. I will never forget the train ride from Western Greece to Athens, the capital. The train was something you would see out of an old 1970's movie (and the year I was in, was 1998). It was compact and traveled about 30 miles an hour. At one point, just to give you an idea of how ridiculous this train was, we hit a small hill and the train was too hot to rev up more to make the one degree climb. So in the middle of the hot dry day, they stopped the train on the slight grade and told us to get off and relax in the desert while the train cooled off. It would only take 30 minutes or so, they told us. So 50 passengers get off in the middle of nowhere in the country of Greece as we start talking in a variety of different languages laughing at the train we are all riding on and wondering why they just don't buy a more powerful locomotive. Obviously we made the best of it and all met each other. The passengers were from everywhere you can think, most being from Australia, South Africa and Canada. I would come to realize on the rest of my trip, that that was who traveled the most during the US' summertime in Europe. After about two hours…yes two hours…we got back on and cheered the train as it tried its hardest to make it up the hill. Thinking back, it might have been easier if all the passengers just got out and pushed. I think we would have saved time and energy that way. But whatever…it's all about the experience right? We eventually made it up the hill and coasted into Athens a few hours later.

I found a hostel, put my stuff down, and slept. Do you see the pattern forming?

I woke up at night. I went out and partied with locals and came back to rest. The next day I made my plan to visit three more islands as I made my way to the sites you need to see in Athens. The Acropolis was amazing. The first thing you realize when you're standing next to the Acropolis is how smoggy the city is below you. The pollution there is unbelievable and I would say unbeatable as far as I have seen. They don't have the same catalytic converter laws there so the emissions from each and every car are unhealthy and sickening. After one day of walking around the city, I felt as if I had smoked a pack of cigarettes and my eyes were watering and stinging as a headache encroached. I found the nearest Internet café to keep in touch with family then went and slept. It was time to leave when I awoke. I found the right ferry and made my way to the first island on my list, Santorini. I will keep this short. If you're going to go to Greece, I recommend spending most of your time on the islands. They are pristine, the beaches are gorgeous, and the people are very nice. From Santorini, I went to Ios. Ios is known for nothing but its parties. I camped out there and met so many travelers. I stayed for 4 nights. I met a girl (who was incidentally Greek and from Athens) there. She had curly hair, a great personality, and a beautiful smile. We spent two days together there and she begged me not to leave. I had to, I would tell her (still not knowing exactly why at the time) and she got sad. I did too, but not as much as her. I was on a mission. Looking back, I know that a girl is what I was really searching for my whole life. I would realize this only later. It wasn't until I met my future wife 10 years later, that it all finally made sense - my wife was actually that partner I had always been looking for my entire life. Lesson in there...

The last island I hit was called Naxos. It was nice. Back to the mainland, I caught the first flight back to Paris. I stayed there one night and took a train to Amsterdam. Yes…you know Amsterdam. Do I even have to tell you about my trip there? I will keep this part out for many reasons and you can experience it for yourself. I am sure you will know what I mean when you go there yourself.

From Amsterdam, I made my way to Germany, stopping in Cologne. It was nice too. From there, I decided to go north of Frankfurt to a little city my uncle lived in. I stayed with him and his family and partied with my cousin one night before leaving to find the great city of Munich, Germany, in an area of the country they call Bavaria. You know when you see a movie of happy Germans drinking beer in a garden and dancing around in tube socks and suspender like outfits? That's what Bavaria and Munich are all about. The city is so laid back and fun that it's worth a full week's stay in my opinion. You can do anything from biking through a nude park, to enjoying a different beer garden everyday, to enjoying the sites and sounds of a blend of nice people and cultures without really running out of anything to do. The hostel I stayed in was great. Just like most of the others, it was large and had a plethora of travelers who all got to know each other very quickly over big beers. I have to say it was one of my favorite stops. After about 3 days there, I decided to see the old communist territory of the Czech Republic and to visit the city of Prague. That was an experience in itself.

The best part of traveling for me is seeing the different types of people out there. I remember the Czech people looking down when they walked, mostly quiet, and humble. I think the Communist regime really took their breaths away and I instantly felt that the people were just trying to get out of that funk as a new republic to find their happiness. The prices were just right for travelers and local merchants to make something of their lives. I helped them significantly with my contributions. You could get a full meal and then some for three American dollars. You could get a beer for less than a dollar and it was a real beer not like the watered down versions you have in the US (Budweiser brand actually started there during the communist years). As far as the people went, everyone was nice. My greatest memory of Prague was the main city train station. You know how here, they play music at the local airport or train station or bus terminal? Well there you are surprised to hear a constant and unchanging beat you would hear in a dark circus coming to town atmosphere. I couldn't describe it more than that but it was so eerie. I felt that a scary looking clown would jump out at anytime, take ahold of me and take me underground to his secret dungeon where they kept all the circus freaks that fed off normal human beings making their way through their territory. Sick? Yeah I know…before judging me…make a trip there and listen to that sound in the train station and then tell me what you feel after experiencing that. Weird stuff…

From Prague, I went to Switzerland. What a beautiful country it was! It was peaceful, beautiful, complex and simple. The people are German, French and Swiss, and I never saw so many Americans as I did in Switzerland. I guess everyone follows the same guidebooks from the US. I had fun adventures there since it's a very outdoorsy kind of culture. If I were to compare it to America, I would say it's like being in the French part of Colorado…well if there was a French part of Colorado.

After 4 days there, in three different cities, it was time to head to Spain. WOW! What a country… The country is beautiful and the people are amazing. It was my favorite country hands down, just above Greece because of the culture and people there. They are very laid back. They eat, sleep, work when they have time, then eat and sleep again. Then wake up at about 8pm to start partying (even the elders) until about 8am the next day. It's the most unstructured culture, but yet the most fun, I had ever encountered. I saw everything from Madrid to southern Spain to the beautiful beaches of Barcelona. It was fantastic. A trip worth making to all, I highly recommend it. I will keep the experience to myself to let you find out for yourself to explore the country and culture for yourself. Book a trip…what are you waiting for?

After two months, I was exhausted and had pictures and memories with me as I made it back to Austin, Texas, where I had finished my studies and left most of my friends to tell them about my unbelievable adventures. Oh yeah, and to be back and get ready to tackle the real world for I was finally ready to settle down for a long-term career now…or so I thought.

12

Clerking around

Following my experience in school where I barely kept my grades up and at the end persuading the dean to let me stay in until graduation, I came up with another bright idea. It was the decision that law school was my cup of tea now and that's what I needed to do next (even though I didn't know anything about the profession and didn't like reading sentences dealing with the law and I hated paperwork, but whatever). So to prove it to myself that the law profession was what I wanted now, I applied everywhere to be a litigation clerk (or runner basically). I diligently persuaded the biggest firm in the city (which was easy because the turnover of clerk jobs was ridiculous I came to learn later) to hire me on the "team". After about a week, I wanted out. I had never seen so much paperwork in my life! Everything needed to be documented, copied, signed, sent out, returned, stamped, filed, taken out, filed again, re-sent while being filed, stamped, stapled, copied, arrrggghhhhhhhhhhhhhhhh!! You get the gist...I thought I was going to learn how to be a lawyer. I didn't learn anything about being an attorney, except that if you are a good bullshitter and you know how to avoid all the necessary paperwork, you will succeed quickly. I found that the key was to get everyone else in the office to do the work for you and for you to just show up semi prepared to court after a great lunch with your mistress, wife, or assistant and talk your way through the process while trying to get as much money for your client or as little money paid out by your client as possible.

I also learned how to sit at a desk all day while trying to find a new excuse, literally almost every other hour, that I could use to persuade my boss to let me go outside of the God forsaken high rise building we were in where there was a constant stream of cold air conditioning going up my nose in a fury, and making me sick everyday I was inside that building. The best part of the job was hanging out with the other clerks and playing on the firm's softball team. I couldn't wait until game night to leave that damn office building and do something physical. Interestingly enough, I still applied to law school while working there and got accepted to a school out in Orange County, California since I wanted to get as far away as possible from everything I knew (first time I had this feeling which I didn't know would return again and again until I stopped it consciously myself 10 years later). The clerk job lasted about 6 months. Before I left, I got my friend hired there who incidentally went on to become a successful lawyer in Houston. I still keep in touch with her until this day. She always reminds me of how I helped her get that job and how she went on to follow her passion in the law (find your passion by the way) and how I used to sit at my desk and look out the window at the firm, at the window washers 15 stories up, and wish I was doing their job instead of the one I was in (even though I am scared of heights, but whatever).

As I was nearing my last days at the firm since I was making everyone mad there because I wasn't working anymore, I got a great call from my friend Mark. It was the call someone like me needed. I had the opportunity to go to Colorado with him and work at a ranch, taking people on horseback riding trips through the mountains. It didn't matter that I had never ridden a horse or knew anything about horses and guiding people through the mountains, but it sounded perfect and it was perfect timing. I sent in my application, he recommended me, and I got the job for $600 a month plus room and boarding. I was mentally in heaven. The only drawback was that I had to wait two months until the summer time. It doesn't seem like much now, but at the time, I pictured myself working at the firm for two more months in that office and realized I wouldn't make it, or they would fire me because they would be fed up with my antics, or I would throw up for the rest of my term there, and none of those options seemed ideal, so I did some investigating. Luckily at the time there was a website called coolworks.com where you can find cool jobs around the country. I found one at a resort in Arizona where they were hiring for only two more months luckily, so I applied online. Two days later, they called me and hired me as a server in their clubhouse. I showed up two weeks later ready to work (and wait on people again, but hey it was in a new place, in the middle of the desert and with new people…what?).

13

Wickenburg, Arizona

As I was looking out the window about to land in Phoenix, Arizona, my heart started beating. I recounted what my dad said to me, before I left, "where the hell are you going? And why?" As I got more nervous thinking of his words, the plane landed and I got my luggage. I walked from the airport, as they told me to do, about 5 miles to the nearest Greyhound station. From there it would be another 2 hours to Wickenburg by bus. Wickenburg is a small charming town of about 30,000 people. One bus station, one horse…just kidding, but you get the gist - it's small.

Once I finally arrived at the bus station there was a gentleman there to pick me up as he had done for all the other workers from all over the US. He was a nice portly man, great guy to take you in for your first day on the job. We discussed the job and what it was like to be out in the middle of the desert, etc. As I unloaded my things, I found my room. In the room next to me, I noticed a loud party going on with workers, I assumed, walking in and out. I dropped my stuff and went next door and introduced myself. There were all kinds of people in there. I saw Northeasterners, Midwesterners, Southerners, and cowboys (who took people on horseback ride trips). I fit in immediately and had fun for the next two months waiting on "well to do" guests that could afford to go out to the desert to a four-star resort in the middle of nowhere for a week. By they way, the food there was amazing. Fresh locks and bagels every morning with hearty breakfasts, lunch, and high quality dinners, it was a great stop on my way up to Colorado to begin my adventures as a Cowboy. On our days off, we would go on bike rides in the desert, take day trips to Phoenix, and go to Mexico when possible. Being that we were on a beautiful golf course, I was able to perfect my swing as well. I met a lot of people there in the short time spent.

14

Howdy Pardners!

Between the Arizona job and the Colorado one, my other friend Jason got married back at home. We had a great time watching my friend tie the knot. After I was done done with the summer, I headed up to Colorado on the adventure of a lifetime with my buddy Mark. My life would never be the same again. It was amazing. We pull up to a small town called Almont. It literally has about 20 people that live there. It's north of Gunnison and south of Crested Butte. It's a beautiful place right in the middle of the mountains. The ranch is called Harmels. Guests from all over the US fly in and spend a week or two in the middle of the mountains to get away from everything the busy city has to offer, and of course to finally get some relaxation time and adventure. Guests could do anything from relaxing on the banks of the river to joining in on cookouts, go on horseback riding trips, or journey down the river on a raft with a guide and other guests. As a worker, I loved being there. There were so many young college aged guys and girls working for the summer and they came from all over. It was a lot like my stint in Arizona. But here I was going to be a cowboy…or at least act like one for three months.

From the first day I got sick because of the altitude. I wasn't used to being so high up in the mountains. It took about a week to get over it and then I was fine. In that week I learned more about horses and the mountains than I could have ever imagined. It was unbelievable. It took me about two weeks of practicing my riding and learning the paths, for the director of the riding program to finally let me take my own ride through the mountains. It was absolutely the best time I had ever had. I would meet people from all over and we would share stories about ourselves. The guests would be so fulfilled at the end of each ride that it was very gratifying to be part of that experience for so many people. We would work hard during the day and then hang out all night with the other ranch workers. For three months, we became a family. We didn't waste any time getting to know each other. The fourth night there, someone decided that we should have a toga party. So we all ended up in togas, boots, and whatever else and had the night of our lives. We were instantly connected and ready for the summer. It only got better from there. The greatest part of that summer was not the money. We were barely getting paid actually. It wasn't the camaraderie, which was really great, but it was the fact that we had an adventure with no real responsibilities and the freedom to experience something many never will. I would recommend working at a resort or ranch to any young (or old person out there). It's highly worth the time and energy you put into it.

Our group "the cowboys and cowgirls" were closer to each other than the others were, and we would wake up every morning and have breakfast together and discuss the work of the day. It was fun. It was five guys and five girls total. We took turns leading trips through the mountains and helping each other out. I can't remember a single time where there was any drama or an absence of real teamwork and loyalty among us all. It was paradise and it was sad when it all came to an end. On my last week there, as I was slowly saying my goodbyes, I went on an overnight camping trip one last time as we had done many times during the season, with a family from California and my friend Mark for one more camping trip together, before my send off to go to law school in California. As luck would happen, the family we took out that night was from San Diego, about an hour and a half from Orange County where I was to be in a couple of months. We took them up about 10,000 feet in the middle of the Rocky Mountains and they had the time of their lives. The family consisted of a gentleman, his wife, and their three daughters. They were mesmerized by the adventure to say the least. As we neared the end of the night, the wife and the girls went to bed and the husband stayed by the campfire with us as we talked about our adventures and stories of where we grew up etc. I went on to tell him that I would be in California soon for law school. He told us about what he did in San Diego and how he had moved there from Northern California. He was telling us about his new company he had created and how he had acquired millions of dollars from CBS, the TV network, as investors in his company and how his website attracted visitors and shoppers, etc. At the time, I remember thinking, huh? I didn't know much about the Internet at that time and what he was doing, but it was interesting nonetheless.

The next day we packed up our things and rode back to the ranch about an hour away. At the end of the trip, the gentleman asked me if I would like to help him with his company for six months until I went to law school since I was going to California anyway. I thought about it and he continued on that he would give me stock options for my time there, and that he and his wife would teach me a lot about sales, marketing and the internet, and then I could go to law school. I would have been crazy to pass up the opportunity. Looking back, I think he could see that I wasn't really that interested in going to law school and he might have seen something else in me, if nothing but a willingness and curiosity to learn and to work. So after about 10 minutes, I said, "Yes…great. Let me know where to show up." I couldn't believe my luck. Wow, I thought to myself, my life was just starting. What an end to the greatest summer…

15

San Diego, California

I had plans to get out to California now and after the ranch, I headed quickly there. It was a liberating and exciting feeling at the same time. I couldn't stop smiling. I was giddy with life. Sun, sand, girls, job, and freedom, how could it be wrong? Once I got there, I found a nice, quiet, and low priced (I got lucky on the first time) apartment and settled in quickly.

Now before I start, I have to say that to this day, this was the second best job I was offered (my first is my current job). Not only was it the greatest time in my life in terms of learning so much, but I also got to live in one of the most beautiful cities we have in this country. The weather in San Diego is, on average, 70 degrees every day with a cool breeze. Now who could get sick of that? When I used to see the weatherman on TV with his weekly forecast, you know with the 7 days laid out with a sun or cloud with lighting, to let you know what the weather was like on that particular day? Well in San Diego, you start to think you are living in the Twilight Zone because every day of the week, of every week, of every month, of every year, there's a weather man coming on the set showing how Monday will be sunny and 70 degrees Fahrenheit, and coincidentally, the same kind of weather will appear on Tuesday, and also for that matter, Wednesday, Thursday, Friday, Saturday, and yes of course, Sunday. The following Monday, the same pattern would start over. The crazy hot weather times were during the summer when it would hit 75 degrees Fahrenheit on a lucky day or even 80 degrees Fahrenheit if winds were coming in from the Eastern California desert. That wasn't all too often though, for the record. On a side note, I think that's why so many people are in shape in southern California. There is always good weather to work out in and to be outside. You actually feel guilty there if you spend time indoors for more than 4 hours since it's nicer outside than it is inside your house, for 99.9% of the time.

On my first day of work, I entered the new offices of a company called Storerunner. It was beautiful and you could tell that the company had put a lot of money into the offices. The great big Storerunner logo, with CBS' initials underneath it, greeted you as you entered. The CEO's wife, who was heading the sales team, greeted me and showed me the ropes. She was the lady that was on the camping trip with him a couple of months before on the overnight camping trip in the mountains, in Colorado. She was excited to see me, as I was her. They had started me on $15/hour and that was more than I had ever made. I thought I was rich already. The goal of the company I worked for was to become the premier online shopping site portal where anyone and everyone would go to get their online shopping done in one place, without the hassle of having to surf to each online merchant's website. For example, if you wanted to buy blue jeans, you could go to Storerunner.com and see a variety of blue jeans from many online merchants including Sears, Gap, Macy's, etc all in one place, so you could pick the one you wanted at the price you were willing to pay. The idea was genius.

My job, as they were trying to get a feel of where I would fit in and help before going to law school, was to call different companies to try to set up a time to talk to one of our sales reps. I had no idea how to do this, but I quickly learned the tricks and the ins and outs. Eventually I was setting the sales reps up with many appointments and was getting bored with my job. I realized that I wanted to sell and make more money. Out of frustration, after about 3 months or so, I asked to be promoted. My boss, the wife of the CEO, quickly said, "I was waiting for you to ask me". I couldn't believe it. Consequently the next week, I started sales training and after about a year I was the top sales rep for the company. I couldn't believe it. I bought a cool jeep and I moved closer to the beach. I was living the high life. I learned a lot and was making a lot of money. I was only 24 years old at the time and I would celebrate by going to Las Vegas (5 hours away). On certain nights we would join the other sales reps and co-workers on the beach for all-night parties and discussions of what we were going to do when we got rich. After a year, things started to unfortunately change towards the negative. During this time, our sales were slowing down and the company started losing money quickly. After two and a half years, Storerunner closed their doors in February of 2001. I was 26. Feeling helpless with no real money, no job, no girlfriend, broken dreams, and one jeep, I headed back to my last home base, Austin Texas. I stayed there for about 6 months living off unemployment checks until I could get back on my feet again. I would never forget the experience I had in San Diego. It was always my plan to make it back there. It never happened but the memories still exist, and the lessons I learned in business and life were well worth the trip there and back.

16

Aloha, can I take your picture please? They're only $12.50 each...

Since I was ready for another adventure after having a "serious job" it was time, in my mind, to escape to a place I had never been before. I saw online that a company was hiring people to take photographs of tourists in Hawaii for the summer. I couldn't believe it. "Is this perfect timing or is this perfect timing?" I remember telling myself. It sounded like the perfect position for someone like me who had just recently experienced the "real world" for two years and wanted an idealistic break in paradise where he could make just enough money to live off until the next decision was made. After a couple of emails back and forth with the owners in Hawaii and a telephone call, I was on my way. They got me a ticket and two weeks later, I was on a plane headed for the great islands in the ocean. I landed about 8 hours after leaving and I was in paradise. It was nighttime when I arrived. Heading for the new apartment they had for me, I was ready to embark on a new journey. When I arrived, there were four young college-aged men there partying, hoopin' and hollerin' with the one that lived there, I think his name was Brad. Brad was the person whom I was taking the place of. Little did I know at the time why Brad was so excited to see me and so excited to leave so quickly. He told me of his time there of over 6 months and how he loved Hawaii but couldn't wait to get back home. Late into the night we crashed and he left the next day. I found myself at noon the next day by myself in an apartment in Hawaii not knowing what to do with myself. Later that afternoon I was supposed to meet my boss. She came by at about 5pm and took me to dinner. We discussed the job and in the next two days she proceeded to teach me everything I needed to know. The gist of the job was this: I was to wake up early every morning, ride my bike to the shore with the camera in the backpack, take pictures of each group of tourists that would show up for a special Pacific Ocean boat ride on a bottomless boat to look at the reefs and what not. There would be 5 trips a day. So that meant that I would have to ride down there (in the hot humid weather) before each trip left for the ocean. I would then arrange all the travelers to take individual and group pictures. Once they boarded the boat, I would then ride my bike back to the apartment (about 2 miles uphill by the way) where I would develop each picture in the computer they had there. After developing the pictures, I would then ride back down to the shore before the boat arrived to try and sell each picture to each tourist once they were back on land. One out of every five tourists would buy a picture - to give you an idea of the huge demand my work would meet (hear the sarcasm?). Once I was done, I would ride back up to the apartment to rest before the next trip. Between boat rides, I got two breaks of about 45 minutes. Eventually I would end up riding up and down the island almost 12 times a day in the hot sun. It was miserable. By the time I would make it back as the sun was setting, I was exhausted. Basically my time in Hawaii, I realized, would not be a nice vacation but a place to slave for owners that were barely making a profit on a mediocre idea. I never had time to see the island while I was there and never had the opportunity to really experience anything Hawaiian. I was so tired each and every day, and all I did was stay inside with the cool air conditioning every chance I could. After about 2 weeks of hell on earth, or what I thought it was, while there I boarded the next plane out and sent the owners a message, "thanks but no thanks". I got back to the mainland in 5 hours landing in LA, wiser and worn out. Lesson learned: if it's too good to be true…it is, trust me. It was time to get a real job again, I told myself. Little did I know that the job market was awful and I would end up in another sort of hell, a loud one in a cult-like atmosphere with a gong.

17

The Gong

Next stop…Hotjobs.com as part of their sales team. Not much to mention here except, once I got there and saw that people had to bang a gong in the office every time they closed a sale, it drove me crazy and I spent half the time covering my ears from this irritation. I lasted two weeks and got the heck out of there. Needless to say, the company is no longer there either. Good riddance…

18

Want a SoBe?

As my short stint on the island and at hotjobs.com ended it was time for me to get a real job, but what happened next was my destiny. It turned out that it was written for me to have more fun and to travel. I was applying to different jobs and I eventually landed one with an event-marketing firm out in Atlanta. They were great and they had just landed a large account, SoBe Beverages. They needed a team to travel around the US together in a nice GMC Tahoe and set up a tent in different locations and hand out SoBe beverages to get the word out on this new drink. That's it…simple as that. We started in California where I met up with the team in San Diego (hello again San Diego it's been so long). We did an event there close to the beach and then headed north to Los Angeles. Once we got to Los Angeles we took care of everyone's thirst on the Santa Monica boardwalk (where I happened to see Meg Ryan by the way) and kept driving north to Northern California. We then went on to Las Vegas, Arizona, to New Mexico where we picked up a new team member since one quit without notice, to the Midwest, over to the East Coast and down to Atlanta to finish off the tour. There wasn't much drama and we got to see a lot of the countryside. There were times the 4 of us would get sick of each other of course and almost wanted to quit ourselves. It did get old and tiresome living out of hotel rooms and eating fast food constantly with no stability. But what the hell, we were young and who cares right? Overall, it was a great opportunity and a lot of fun. This experience led me to start the process of thinking of a new idea that would eventually become the first business I created.

19

Surf Break!

Being on the road is not easy. You pack light, eat horribly, and sleep even worse. But one thing I got from my travels in doing event marketing was that I had my first aha! moment on my entrepreneurial journey. While traveling it seemed we needed Internet at all times and I was never able to connect for free or even find a computer that had Internet. Of all the hotels we would stop at, only half at the time had some sort of public computer (this was 2001). Once my travels were over, I headed back to Austin Texas. I worked at the airport for America West airlines until I could find my next gig or real job. Neither one came, hence I eventually just created my own company.

I noticed the high traffic airport in Austin at the time didn't have computers for the travelers to check their email or surf the Internet. This idea perplexed me for sometime and it had started back when I was on the road promoting SoBe beverages. I thought that there must be a need by others out there for Internet on the go as there was for me. So I just put my plan on paper and set up a meeting with the administration folks at the Austin airport. They liked the idea at first but couldn't figure out a way to implement it in the actual airport. So I got creative and started talking to existing tenants to see who would partner with me.

The first company I talked to was a food hosting company that had the rights for all restaurants in the airport. After our first meeting, we were moving forward. We had plans in place, paperwork drawn up and everyone was enthusiastic and on the same page, up until the very end. The idea was that I was going to rent some space in one of their open area seating grills in the middle of the airport where users could come by and surf the Internet. Everyone was on board except the very last decision maker who happened to reside in Buffalo NY. He looked at the plans and said sorry, this wasn't something they were going to pursue at this time and of course we could revisit it later. It turns out that this executive didn't want to take the chance to rent out a small portion of his space for this service. This wasn't taken very well by me to say the least. I walked around the airport about to give up on the entire thing and called the airport contacts, telling them it's not going to work out. They told me ok, if you get anyone to partner with you let us know, even if it's the airlines. Right then and there my mind started racing with the idea of partnering with an airline…who would it be? How would it work? When can we talk?

After considering it more for a couple of days I approached the Southwest Airlines customer service Manager and pitched the idea to her. She loved it. Eventually, I put the plan together again, customized it for Southwest Airlines, and set up a meeting between the airport and us to discuss the next steps. Afterwards, everyone was on board and we moved it up the ladder to the headquarters to get it signed off by their marketing and property departments. After going back and forth and almost losing the entire deal again, they finally agreed (due to my undying persistence and a very smart looking financial spreadsheet my brother put together for me) and I was on my way. Later on I remember a lady in the property department asking me how the heck I got this thing approved and under way and I just smiled and said, hard work and with your help of course (which is the first time I realized that anything is possible if you are diligent, persistent, work hard, and you find the right customers and solution). So the idea was to place Internet stations in one Southwest Airlines boarding area to allow their customers, while waiting for their planes, to use the Internet. Of course this was at a time when there weren't a lot of mobile Internet solutions or phones for that matter, with good browsers on them, and laptops were more expensive and were less prevalent than they are these days (this was in 2002). So I didn't have any idea how to get this done of course, but like they say, accept the job and then figure out how to do it. That's just what I did. I partnered with a local technology company to build the computers and situate them in airport specs by embedding them into shelves that looked like the surrounding airport. So they actually looked like they were part of the airport on purpose. And of course, since I didn't have any money to do this, in return for helping me get this thing off the ground the company got free branding from the high traffic of travelers that came through the airport every day. It turned out to be the most fun I have ever had. I met so many people including new partners, investors, other business people and entrepreneurs and a lot of other folks that worked in the airport as well. In fact, I once needed a ticket badly and one of my new friends at Southwest Airlines gave me her buddy pass so I could travel. I will always be grateful for her caring deed. From there I went on to partner with American Airlines and even find a partner for the St. Louis airport. Eventually though, laptops dropped in price and phones had better browsers to surf the Internet. Suddenly, Internet stations weren't as popular as they once were so I had to close my business down. But it was definitely the most fun and positive experience I had ever had. And I must add that I was able to leave a lasting impression, which feels really good. What I mean is, from the display of my embedded computers, Southwest Airlines eventually went on to use the similar concept of creating laptop stations that were the same idea and colors as the surrounding boarding areas that we used with Surf Break, where people could use and charge their laptops to surf the internet (instead of being a computer station) while waiting to board their planes. So I helped create an environment that many travelers traveling on Southwest Airlines experience, even as we speak, to this day. Next time you fly Southwest Airlines and see the boarding area with the laptop station think of me will you?

20

More stops along the way...

After the closing of my business I was ready to start anew. What direction was I headed for? I had no clue. It's funny how things work out and how you never quite know where you're going to go. After a few weeks, and I don't recall the details, I somehow hooked up with a family friend that had just opened a chain of restaurants. He needed a manager and I needed a job, and given my previous experience at Chili's I figured it would be fine, so I was hired. Long story, short…I didn't last long there given the fact, which I of course remembered later, that I don't like working with food and don't like working in a restaurant, which by the way is much harder than it looks. As with everything though, I am grateful for the experience. From there I thought back to my days sitting on the couch with my mom watching the Love Boat on TV and how fun that seemed to be, so I went and got a cruise ship social host job. Unfortunately, that job only lasted one day when I suddenly realized in horror that I would be stuck in a room the size of a bedroom closet (I'm not kidding…you had to walk in sideways when there were two of you in the room at the same time and each room held 3 people) in the middle of the ocean on the bottom deck of a huge ship with no windows to see out of. I had an anxiety attack, grabbed my things, and told the captain I was not setting sail with them into the sunset that night. Following that slight heart attack, I went back home to Texas, tried my hand at graduate school, nighttime event marketing for a cigarette manufacturer, selling furniture, teaching special education students (which was intrinsically rewarding but really tested my patience unfortunately) and back into sales for a great company until I got to my favorite job of all and it's where I currently work…a communication industry manufacturer as a territory manager where I take care of sales, marketing, business development and customer service. I am very happy…do you know why? Because I use my natural talents and my passion to create positive relationships every day of the week, every month, and every year. Everything I have ever done previously to this job has set me up with the experience to be able to fully handle this job on all levels. And I am happy. I love my job, the company I work for, and helping others at the same time.

I hope the same thing happens for you if it hasn't already, and I hope my little life journey put a smile on your face and made you think of what you'd like to do. If anything, I hope it helped you take a break and just mentally participate in a wacky adventure.

Note: What you don't know will not hurt you… That's what I learned. Through the adventures and people I've met, I would say that nothing is that different from where I started. But I had to find out for myself. This is something I'd like to share with you. Many of you might be wondering just what that next stop is for you. Some of you might be wondering what that next place has that this one doesn't. Some of you might be wondering…what if I had made that decision long ago, would my life be different now? And many of you I know are thinking what do I want to do?

I'm here to tell you. You can take the long way or the short way…but one thing's for sure, you get back to where you started, no matter what. The short way is just as mentally long as the long way for sure. Advice: Find what you would like to do and what you could live with doing every day… as opposed to who you want to be right away, and you might find the answer quicker than you think.

AND: If you have come this far and would like to keep in touch and/or ask a question or seek advice please email me anytime at tareknh@gmail.com.

Have fun on the journey and stay positive – TH

21

I want that job now! Step by step guide

STEP 1 - FIND THE DECISION MAKER

Find the Decision Maker...As with the sales process in selling a product or service, this is the same step, but with a different product—you. What you think generally differentiates you from another qualified candidate is not what really differentiates you from him/her. It has nothing to do with your name, color of skin, religion, qualifications (if they're fairly the same or if they're looking to fill the position with someone who is willing to learn), or how long your resume or cover letter is. It has nothing to do with how you type or the school you went to. However the email address you send it to has a significant effect on how you get treated after the matter.

One lesson I learned early on in the job hunting game, which they don't teach you in school or in career books, is that individual passion, contact research, persistence, and your own unique way of expressing yourself towards your dream job, play a larger part in gaining the attention of your desired employers than anything else.

Sales is an industry which I feel everyone should have the experience of being a part of. The reason for this is because it teaches you how to approach the process of gaining things that are hard to have. It teaches you how to supply the company or as in this case, the employer, with the information they desire from you to close the deal.

In the sales process, you deal with certain steps towards accomplishing your goals. A great salesperson will use his experience and apply it to the company he's prospecting. But before he can do that, he needs the most important factor—the decision maker (also known as the DM) in the company, to which he will sell his product, in your case, yourself. This person can be the VP of Marketing, the CEO, the VP of Sales, the Director of Product Development, etc. It depends which department you are looking to get into. If you don't have the proper decision maker, you don't have a chance. Anyone other than this person will be a waste of your time for whatever it is you're trying to accomplish.

Finding the DM is easily done with the internet. These days, the company you're trying to get an interview with almost always has a website somewhere on the internet. In fact there's probably a 99% chance that they have a website for their company. This is the quickest and best way to learn all there is to know about the company and its open positions. Not to mention this is a great way to learn about the leaders of the company as well—a very important tool in acquiring your dream job.

Once you see a job you are qualified for or somewhat qualified for, take the time to research the company and its products, leaders, job openings, etc. From this you will get a summarized idea of what the company is all about. You can find all of this information on the company's website.

Surfing the internet can be a long, painful process, or an easy, quick research tool if you're using it in a focused manner. When, for example, you get a prospective company in mind and you decide you have found the position you want to be considered for, then research the site. You can pretty much always guess the company's web address by using their name and adding the dot com ending. For example Gap would be Gap.com. Sears would be Sears.com, etc. If that doesn't work, then you can go to Yahoo.com or Google.com or any other search engine, and type in the company's name. *9 times out of 10* you will get that company's website through the search results.

After finding the company's website, you will see for yourself all the links on there to learn all about the company. If for some reason, the DM's are not included as one of the links, you can always go to Hoovers.com and type in the company's name and it will bring up the company's executives for

you as well (on top of supplying the physical address, phone number, company history/story, and its website URL).

So for example, if you are looking to apply for a marketing position, find out who the head of marketing is for that company. If it's not listed on the website or on Hoovers.com, then call the company's front desk (a research tool which will help you learn a lot about the inter-workings and executives of the company as well). If the front desk person will not give you the information or will not transfer you, ask to be transferred to that person's assistant. They will always allow you to do this, since they need to have a professional image to display.

After you have found out who that person is, find out what their email is for human resources as well. You can usually find this out on the website under the jobs or employment section of the site. To be overly proactive, finding the name and contact info (email most importantly) for the head of Human Resources will help out greatly as well.

One important factor to remember is if you are looking to apply for a Marketing Manager position for example, your best bet will be to find out the head of marketing's info like the VP of Marketing. If he/she doesn't exist, then what is the highest position within that department? It might be the Director of Marketing. If there is no one else above your desired position (as in many small companies), then find out the CEO's name and contact info. The purpose of this is so you can get your information to the leaders of the company or your department so they can see your passion, persistence, resourcefulness, and desire (above other candidates who are just applying through the Human Resource department) for the position they are looking to fill. Once they see your information, they either keep it for themselves or trickle it down to their subordinates and/or the human resource department. The latter will happen most of the time. This is good. Even though this seems like a long way of getting your resume to the proper person, you will actually see that there is an advantage to this. As in the sales process, a product from your company or a prospective candidate, as in this case, that is forwarded from a highly positioned executive of the same company, will *9 times out of 10*, get the call for the interview from Human Resources than someone else who applied for the same position the "correct" way. Sound crazy? It's true, as you will see for yourself.

This is what sales professionals know for a fact. Now you do too!

After you have found the DM of your prospective company, there comes the process of figuring out his/her email address, the most powerful tool you have in acquiring your desired job.

Note: Linkedin.com is also a great resource for this step

STEP 2 - EMAIL "CODE-BREAKING"

What's her email address? I sure would love to contact her. Ever felt like this? Me too—we all have. This chapter will explain how you go about the process of getting the email address of the DM you are trying to get a hold of for a particular job. This is the most important step in the entire process because without this, you are lost in the pile of rubbish that is made up of everyone else's resumes. Email is the most powerful tool where average prospects like you and I can get a hold of a powerful company executive. One thing you can count on is this: Even company executives check their email. They might not answer the phone, open their mail, pick up the fax, or check their voicemails, but they DO CHECK THEIR EMAILS!

Just a short note before we get started. The #1 reason that this is the most important step is because once you forward your resume to the appropriate leader, *9 times out of 10*, you have put your life in the hands of an ambitious, loyal, dedicated to the bright future of his/her company, professional. They hold that position for a reason. They love to see passion for their company. Trust me. Not to generalize, but many human resource personnel that you send your

resume don't usually sense the motivation or react

as quickly on your behalf, because that's not how they would do things, 9 times out of 10. They get hundreds to thousands of the same kinds of formatted resumes every week. Why would yours stick out? They don't know you from another. They don't see the little qualities that will make you stand out above the crowd. It's the truth! That's why most qualified resumes get "dumped" (unless you know someone). That's why you always have to get ahold of the DM in YOUR potential department. That person will sense your desire, persistence, and potential more.

Even though this is the most important step, you will not just send your resume to the department of choice of course… It's always good to send the same email to the Human Resource department as well, as to keep with the proper procedures of the company's hiring policy. As explained earlier, you will already have the human resource email address that you get from the website. *9 times out of 10,* it will be

jobs@company.com, employment@company.com, humanresources@company.com, or hr@company.com.

(Just a word of advice here for your resume. It will be wise to include the future position's title or job requirements in the details of your last job description on your resume. This way you will

show your experience with the position you are trying to get into. It will be advantageous for you to put the company name and the position you're looking to get into at the top of your resume in your "objective" statement as well. Companies love seeing their name up there).

One thing I have learned from past experience while using email is that almost every employee's email is formatted the same within the same company. *9 times out of 10,* the executive or DM you are trying to get ahold of has the same format as the entire work force in the same company, including the CEO! Let's create the scenario of an applicant to show how this will work. For this example we'll use "Bob." Bob is applying for the "Product Manager" position for let's say, "company AB". Bob is somewhat experienced in product management from his last company even though his title was "Business Development Associate." Just as well, this new position is the position of his dreams. This is the job he wants. Bob has already found out the company's information and its decision makers within the different departments of the company, by doing research on the website and contacting the front desk. He found that the Product Manager position is under the Product Development department category. Product Development has a Vice President as its head. This is the DM. This DM happens to be "Lucy Powers." She is the highest person in this department. Lucy is the person Bob will email with his resume, professional reference letter, and picture (optional). Just a note on the picture: A picture is never necessary (as any employer will make sure to tell you out loud), but it helps in determining your professional appearance, etc which they might be wondering in the back of their minds. Also this is a good way to make you stick out from the rest*. Even though this might seem untraditional, it's the truth. What you don't know sometimes hurts you.

(* Do not send a picture if applying for any job in the entertainment industry. This is looked upon as unprofessional and negatively by the company. They see this as a back-way into the company with the desire to become a future actor/director/agent and they will toss it all out immediately.)

Moving on, the rule of thumb with emails is this: Unless you were lucky enough to find out the DM's email address via a call or by researching the website, you will have to be creative in sending the email to the proper address. It's very easy. In the "to" section of your email, you will have to put all the combinations of that person's name before the @ sign in the email.

In this case, Bob knows two things for sure. 1) The DM is Lucy Powers *and* 2) the company's website is www.companyab.com. *9 times out of 10,* this is the domain of the email server for that company as well (@companyab.com). From here Bob can format his cover letter in the body of his email and attach his resume, professional reference letter(s), and picture. In the "subject" line, he will put "Product Manager position" or Job # (if there's a job # under the listing on the website). In the "to" line, since he knows the company's URL is @companyab.com, he needs to include every professional email name format he can think of, before the @ sign, since he doesn't know her email address directly. It will look like this:

Lucy.Powers@companyab.com, LucyPowers@companyab.com, Lucy_Powers@companyab.com, LucyP@companyab.com, Lpowers@companyab.com.

This way he covers all the main, professional formats of email addresses used by 99% of the companies out there now. Of course, 1% of the time, you will see that some executives don't use one of these formats or even domain (@companyab.com). They might use the lastname.firstname@, or lastname.first initial @, or last initialFirst name@ or first initialLast initial@, etc. Or some companies might use a totally different domain name for the email server. Most of the time this not the case. In cases such as these, you might have to do more investigating over the phone. If the front desk attendant won't give you the email and won't transfer you to the DM, ask to be transferred to the DM's assistant. Tell the assistant you would like to send her an email that she can forward to the DM. *9 times out of 10,* whatever email domain and format she gives you for her, that's what the DM's email is. At this point, if you still can't get the DM's email address, just forward to the assistant since you already asked her nicely if she wouldn't mind forwarding your email to the DM anyway. *9 times out of 10,* they will do this for you.

Once the email is sent, depending on your email server, you will get back a message saying "undeliverable" or "unknown host" or something else that will tell you your email didn't reach <u>ALL</u> of its destinations. Once you open that email and see which email addresses it <u>didn't</u> get sent to, you can rule out which email format that DM and probably everyone else in the company has. As in this example, Bob might get an

email back saying "undeliverable" in the subject line and the body saying these addresses were *"undeliverable"* :

Lucy.Powers@companyab.com, LucyPowers@companyab.com, Lucy_Powers@companyab.com, LucyP@companyab.com.

So by process of elimination, Bob knows that Lucy's email is Lpowers@companyab.com, and that she did get the email he sent her. This is a great confirmation for you as well as a new period of excitement when you're going after your dream job, knowing your potential boss has just received your resume and information on their screen. You'll see!

And as a quick note, most of America's companies today use one of these three formats for their company emails: firstname.lastname@, or firstname_lastname@, or firstinitialLastname@. In addition to this, once you find out the format you can pretty much assume that the head of human resources has the same format if you would like to find out their name as well, from the website or front desk. This may be tricky, but once you figure out a contact, the email is a piece of cake. One tip when doing this—if you encounter a front desk

attendant who will not forward you to anyone in human resources (HR), just get transferred again to the assistant of the DM and ask her to transfer you to HR. The assistant will happily do this most of the time. Once this is done, if no one answers in HR, you will get the voicemail of someone in HR and you can now hear their name and send them an email with the same format, or leave them a message to call you back (but be sure to write down their name).

Right before you guess the email address though, you need a unique cover letter in the body of your email. Unique, I mean, only in the way of you.

STEP 3 - JUST BE YOURSELF

In my experience in dealing with the "career professionals" out there or the "right career books" with tips on writing your cover letter, most are below satisfactory and generalize too much. They are structured and don't do that much for you. Even though having certain ways of accomplishing things is a great guide, in the end you need to take that learning and MOLD it into your own unique way of going about it. As in this case, take the format of a cover letter that you've read from these books and apply them, IF YOU WANT TO. If you don't, don't. The only important rule in forming your cover letter in the body of the email is this: Just Be Yourself. You need to stand out!

This is really easy to do considering you, more than anyone else, know yourself, your passions, why you want this particular job, and what you can add. Here is a recommendation and example is this (Of course there will be differences in your cover letter based on your unique personality):

First Paragraph:_Introduction and history

Example-

"Hello Ms. Lucy Powers:

How are you? I wanted to introduce myself and tell you how passionate I am about the Product Manager Position you have posted on your website. I know how to be the best candidate for this job. I have been interested in CompanyAB for some time now and have done significant research on it and the industry. I know that I can be a great addition to the team where you will definitely see my ambition, loyalty, leadership, enthusiasm, desire to succeed, and goal to be a team player.

Note: This is an example of an informal way to get the reader's attention. The DM will sense your uniqueness, tone and enthusiasm. (Enthusiasm is a big factor in getting the interview.)

Second Paragraph:_Experience

In my last job, I created and implemented various programs for "CompanyZ" as their Business Development Associate. I introduced and carried out monthly promotions, weekend radio events, and the "high stakes" link on our website. There I learned to work as a team to get things accomplished, as well as to be a leader in the product mangement/development role. I have 3 + years of product management experience as well as 2 years of internet industry experience. I am looking to learn more and as much as possible to be a future leader for your great company.

Note: Make sure you add the fact that you want to learn as much as possible. This is one thing companies love. On top of that they want to know that you are interested in their company and you want to STAY and become a future leader for them. This shows them your ambition and loyalty, both very important.

Third Paragraph: Closing

I know what it's like to be part of a startup and dynamic company. That's the main reason I am interested in companyAB on top of everything else. I know how to be a great fit and that once you meet me and see my passion and desire to be part of your team, you will want me to join.

Note: Let them feel that they are missing out if they don't meet you.

Can we discuss today? I can interview right away and start ASAP once you feel there's a fit.

Thanks for your time and I look forward to hearing your thoughts on this real soon.

Note: Always let them know you are available immediately (even if you have to give a two-weeks notice—they understand that already) and always ask them if you can discuss this week. Always thank them for their time and make sure you let them know that you can't wait to hear from them <u>soon</u>.

Sincerely,

Bob Rogers

555-555-5555 cell

bobrogers@youremail.com

--Resume, Professional Reference Letter, and Picture attached

Note: Add what you've attached and the best ways you can be reached (as in this case, cell phone number and email address).

It can be short and to the point (remember: these executives don't have a lot of time and they appreciate the quick message).

After you have created and sent your email, you will have to send the same one to the Human Resources department to show you followed the rules of their employment procedures. This is no problem—just cut and paste the body, and attach the same attachments and send it again to human resources (ex. HR@companyab.com). I don't recommend sending the same email to both email addresses at the same time. It's better to let them be separate so the DM doesn't delete the email because he/she assumed that HR took care of it, or the other way around.

STEP 4 – FOLLOW UP PHONE CALL AND THANK YOU!

After you have sent your email for the job, wait one business day. If you haven't heard from them, follow up. In this case, Bob will call and ask the front desk attendant if he can talk to Ms. Lucy Powers. *9 times out of 10*, because of her position, the front desk attendant will forward Bob to Ms. Powers' voicemail (or assistant) instead of directly to Ms. Powers. So Bob will leave a message enthusiastically and passionately telling how he is very interested in this job and how he looks forward to discussing it soon. Don't be afraid of this step, the people in these positions love persistence. That's the key to getting the job you want—as it is while trying to sell any product to any company, in sales generally. If you still haven't heard back from the DM a week after you sent the email (five business days), then it's recommended you call the DM again. If she has an assistant, find out when the DM will be back and if she can get the DM to call you or help with the application process for this job. GREAT assistants are always looking to help, that's why they're there. Remember that! If there is no assistant, leave another message for the DM. At that point space your calls to every two to three days, as to be persistent but not annoyingly persistent. Trust me –a real leader will take your calls in a positive manner. Actually, a real leader would have gotten back to you in two days, which will probably happen 70% of the time. Give it a try, you'll see!

If for some reason, you have not heard back from the DM or the Human Resources department after a week, then while you're leaving messages for the DM, make sure to call the HR department and get someone on the phone there or through email (as discussed earlier). Hopefully it won't ever get that far. The key to this chapter is **Persistence**. You have to be persistent until they give you a solid yes, let's move forward/interview, or a solid no, sorry not now or we're not interviewing/hiring for this position any longer.

And finally after you have had the interview for your dream job and they just love you, make sure to send a "thank you email" to the DM and the Human Resources department (and anyone else you interviewed with) for their time and let them know that you look forward to working with them in the future and being part of the team. Important step! This shows your professionalism and continued persistence. Sound too good to be true? Try it out, you'll see for yourself!

These 4 steps just outlined are the only tools you need in acquiring your dream job interview. Simply, this is the sales process summarized and applied to the job search. This is the same technique that sales professionals use in their daily procedures, as well as other areas of their lives. It works for them, and it will work for you!

Whether one is looking for that executive level, mid-level, or entry-level position, this short guide will help any working professional tremendously, as they travel down their career path in search of their dreams. Make sure to keep this guide with you as you change careers in the future!

© 2018 Tarek N Hassan